the GET NOTICED notebook

a crash course on leadership for
people feeling invisible at work

BECKY GRANINGER

authorHOUSE

AuthorHouse™
1663 Liberty Drive
Bloomington, IN 47403
www.authorhouse.com
Phone: 833-262-8899

Published by AuthorHouse 02/16/2022

ISBN: 978-1-6655-5146-5 (sc)
ISBN: 978-1-6655-5145-8 (hc)
ISBN: 978-1-6655-5144-1 (e)

Library of Congress Control Number: 2022902607

PREFACE

There is no excuse for lackluster process management or poor people skills. This handbook is a crash course—a practical dictionary, if you will—on the strengths needed to achieve positive leadership.

It isn't theory but practice. Most entries are short and to the point, and these strengths are universal enough to apply to almost any leadership situation.

I wish I could tell you that only good leaders get noticed.

Unfortunately, we see strong personalities move ahead even when they have deficits in knowledge or skill. Accept that fact, but focus on how you can perform at the best of your own capabilities.

Draw attention to yourself, without losing your soul.

CONTENTS

RED FLAG

Has this ever happened to you? Someone else says what you've been saying, and this time, everyone listens to the other guy.

It could be how you're saying it, it could be your lack of authority, it could be that the other person has a stronger peer network or that people simply like him better, but regardless, this is a sign that you have a problem. If it happens a lot, you have a big problem, and that problem can be described as *invisibility*.

There are many reasons for feeling invisible, from things that are in your control to the many that aren't. Even those not within your control must be dealt with.

The reality is that it's easy to become invisible—to become stuck, to watch others pass you by, to be dominated by a bad boss, or to feel irrelevant or even used.

You can hope for something to change, or you can change. If you are an invisible person, the big three changes you should consider making are to change your work habits, change your attitude, or change your job.

Set a goal of becoming visible and therefore more valuable.

YOUR VISIBILITY QUOTIENT

Let's see how visible you are by answering these easy, yes-or-no questions:

Have you gotten a promotion in the last eighteen months?

Do you have a best friend at work?

Do you have a great relationship with your boss? Not *good*, but *great?*

Do you have a mentor?

Have you received an above-average raise in the last twenty-four months?

Are you currently on any special task forces or committees?

Does your boss's boss know your first name?

Are you involved with industry trade groups or associations?

Have you survived a recent layoff?

Do you socialize with coworkers outside of work?

Do you love what you do?

Do you intentionally eat lunch at your desk?

Do you ask questions in meetings?

Are you an extrovert?

Do people describe you as nice?

Have you ever been published, or have you participated in a high-profile internal or external event representing your department or your organization?

Are you comfortable correcting bad behavior within your team?

Have you referred a friend as a new hire?

Do people describe you as smart?

If you answered *no* to more than ten questions, then you need to evaluate your work persona.

Figure out a way to become more visible.

TAKING STOCK

You need to be visible—for the right reasons, of course—and to do that you need to network at multiple levels. That includes peers, subordinates, and senior managers.

You need an effective working relationship with your boss, and you need to develop a relationship with your boss's boss, because he or she has significant impact on your upward mobility and remuneration.

Speaking for myself, I have been fortunate in that I've had the opportunity to work for many good leaders. I think I'm a good "picker" of bosses, but I recognize that it's much harder to judge your boss's boss. Much of the time, that relationship is pivotal to your long-term success. Your immediate boss affects your daily life, but your boss's boss affects your direction, your resources, and usually your salary.

Without exception, you need to be comfortable speaking up in meetings. This is a skill that even introverts need to master.

You also need to look the part. Creative positions allow for the most leeway in dress, so use it to telegraph your confidence and vibe. Don't be the frumpiest or the trendiest in your group, but make the most of what you've got. Even just the title of Barbara Corcoran's book, *If You Don't Have Big Breasts, Put Ribbons on Your Pigtails*, lets you see what I mean.

Develop your own personal style. It will help you stand out.

WORKING MANAGERS

Today's managers juggle their traditional job roles and personal lives, and now do so with ever-expanding workloads and 24/7 organizational contact.

They exist in the middle. Those above them impose strategies that need implementation, and those below look to them for direction and support.

No longer is the middle manager a pure manager. Many have responsibilities for individual tasks as well as supervising others. Due to the general flattening of many organizations' hierarchies and reductions in overall staff size, even managers of managers have individual tasks and projects to complete.

Middle managers are important to the success of any organization. They aren't the butts of jokes anymore. In fact, the relationships between these managers and the employees who report directly to them significantly affect motivation, productivity, satisfaction, and retention.

However, middle managers are a stressed bunch, and many feel like they don't have an advocate. They work inside organizations with cultures defined by doing more with less. With so much pressure, many feel they don't have time to carry out all their duties as effectively as they wish they could, and many don't get the training they need to be good people managers.

Look for ways to improve your skill in getting work done through others.

REAL LIFE

Working long hours seriously affects one's ability to enjoy the myriad of responsibilities and activities of one's personal life. Frankly, most people don't make enough to hire personal assistants, nannies, chefs, and fitness trainers to help them manage their lack of personal time.

We often fall into the trap of believing that we have to invest more time at work in order to move forward. We value moving forward, because it means more money and more rewarding work.

The snare is that this time investment constantly expands. *Work through lunch, come in early, or stay late. Or come in early* and *stay late. Work on Saturdays.*

The ever-expanding work week is similar to and possibly linked to the other trap: the more money you make, the more you spend. Spending up to your level of income becomes a self-fulfilling prophecy.

My real-life advice is to put a time limit on your work week. Focus on what you deliver and not the hours you log. Learn to truly prioritize and delegate.

Learn to say no.

IN THE MIDDLE

Working managers are *sandwich* managers. They nurture and grow their staff and support their own manager's needs, all while getting their own work done.

The reality is that all managers are sandwich managers, and the higher you go in an organization, the more time you will have to spend managing up. Many managers, while adept at motivating and anticipating the needs of their direct reports, overlook the importance of building strong relationships with their own supervisors.

If you work for a difficult person, it can be hard to develop an effective relationship. Your approach for dealing with your difficult boss may depend on the level of interaction. Is your daily life a torment, or do you simply receive a dose of crazy once a week or once a month? One suggestion is to grin and bear it. If you can hold on to your sense of self-worth, then putting up with a jerk may be the most expedient choice—meaning you can wait him or her out.

You can also try to develop a relationship with an inside mentor, ideally with someone who is equal to or more senior to your boss, who can help you learn coping skills and counteract your bad boss's machinations.

I hate bullies. If your boss is one, or if his or her boss is one, you have a big problem. The only way to counteract a bully is with someone with more power. The tricky part is that these guys often exhibit their bullying behavior to those below them in the pecking order and exhibit toadying behavior to those above them.

First, learn how to deal with the stress. Exercise is one method. I have one friend who boxes, and on the other end of the spectrum, I have another who does yoga. Then, make sure you have a confidant. You need someone to talk to who can give you advice.

When stress is related to a work relationship, start by evaluating your reaction to the situation. Is it possible that you are making things worse?

Only you can decide how you are going to interact with your manager. It is an active decision, and it can impact your future trajectory.

WATCH YOUR STEP

It is interesting to watch people travel on escalators. Some people grip the handrail; others avoid it. Many stumble as they get on or off, either because of a misstep or a distraction. Many stand still, comfortable with being moved along with the others, while some step quickly ahead.

Your career is like an escalator. Just because an escalator is working the way it's designed to, that doesn't make it safe. It requires riders to pay attention.

You have to make smart choices.

To move ahead you have to work hard, but to be really successful you have to work smart. I know this sounds like a platitude.

Let's say you are a proposal reviewer for your firm, and your input results in a close rate which is twenty percent more than any other reviewer. You often stay late to work on as many proposals as possible. You are recognized for your expertise, and you are proud of that fact. However, if you were to change your focus from staying late and working on individual proposals to teaching others to do what you do, your company could generate a lot more business, and you would expand your impact and gain an enhanced reputation.

It is easy to be busy, but pay attention, because it is possible that things you are doing may not be helping you strategically advance your current situation or your career.

FAILURE TO LAUNCH

Four frogs were sitting on a lily pad. Three decided to leave. How many were left?

The answer is four. Just because they decided to leave doesn't mean they actually left. Nonperforming behavior happens all the time. Often the culprit is that one person who made a decision for someone else to implement, or the guy in charge who didn't figure out what the team needed in order to accomplish the task. People themselves make decisions they never execute for all kinds of reasons. Maybe they don't have the skill, the authority, or the time to do it. Maybe they are afraid of failure, or they procrastinate. Maybe they get distracted as new obstacles crop up or new priorities are set.

Four of the biggest reasons for lack of execution are poor communication skills, prioritization issues, risk aversion, and lack of vision. To succeed, you have to bring your team along. You need to manage limited resources (people, time, and money). You have to take risks, and you need to know where you're going. This applies to every level and layer of management.

Since I wrote this section, I discovered *Five Frogs on A Log: A CEO's Field Guide to accelerating the transition in Mergers, Acquisitions, and Gut Wrenching Change*, by Mark L. Feldman and Michael F. Spratt. My usage of the frog metaphor applies to any business dealing with change and focuses on implementation.

Plans must be translated into actions, and quickly.

CAREER SAVVY

Let me tell you an old navy yarn. At his retirement gala, a departing admiral was asked what contributed to his successful career. His answer was two words: *good choices*. The junior officer inquired about the basis for those choices. The admiral's single word answer was *experience*. The junior officer persisted: *how did you gain that experience?* The answer came back: *bad choices*.

There is no substitute for experience, but I suggest you also take advantage of others' experiences. Not all bad choices have to be ones you make yourself. Talk to others, read, observe, and listen.

The strengths identified in this book revolve around communication, team-building, and conflict resolution. They are geared towards healthy leadership, not win-at-all-costs practices.

Pick a few to focus on, and then use them to your advantage as you work to stand out. Combinations and emphases will change based on the culture of a particular organization, your own personal makeup and objectives, and the needs of the people around you. After that, set a goal of becoming a good guy and an effective leader. The two are not mutually exclusive.

Do the right thing is a motto to live by. Be true to yourself and your organizational responsibilities. Keep your promises. Don't get distracted. Don't take shortcuts. Care about your customers and your employees, and don't sacrifice the long term for the short term unless absolutely necessary.

Constantly evaluate your actions—don't tarnish your integrity.

WRONG TURNS

We have all taken a wrong turn—on the road and in life.

Think of how you react. If you are in the car, the wrong turn may make you nervous. Will you get lost? Will you get stuck in traffic? How will you get back to where you were? Do you blame the other person in the car?

Context is everything. If the wrong turn puts you in a scary neighborhood, you will react differently than if you're in a familiar and safe location. A wrong turn with no exit ramp is a lot different than a swing around the block. If you're running late for an appointment, that wrong turn now intensifies your anxieties, as compared to a day with plenty of time when that wrong turn becomes an opportunity to explore a new area.

The same reactions apply to life changes. Face it, we don't always make the right job decisions, vacation choices, relationship connections, investment picks, or volunteer selections. If we did, we would be perfect, and that isn't possible. We do the best we can with the information we have at the time. The key is to recognize when a "turn" you've made may not be the right one, and then to decide what to do.

If you dwell on wrong choices too often, you will never get ahead, because you will be mired in "woulda coulda shoulda."

Understand the warning signs that may have been there, so you don't make the same mistake twice.

POSSIBILITIES

You can exponentially grow yourself and your team if you focus on performance as well as positive leadership, innovation, and change. The good news is that—after years of businesses focusing on consolidation, cost control, and technology—companies are now turning their attention toward strategic issues of innovation and growth, to which people are the key.

In mathematics, for any exponentially growing quantity, the larger it gets, the faster it grows. The same principle applies to people. Winning teams win more. Successful leaders become more successful. Profitable companies become more profitable.

Be open to new ideas and ways of working, because that will lead to new opportunities.

ACCEPT RESPONSIBILITY

My son frequently uses the expression, "man up," usually accompanied by a derisive snort. It basically means *take responsibility, and accept the consequences of your actions.*

I use it to remind managers that they are supposed to *manage,* to make and execute decisions, to hold people accountable—and yes, to support their bosses.

Promoting a wonderful worker to manager is one of the largest and most frequently repeated organizational human-resources mistakes. Just because a person can do a specific job well doesn't mean he or she can manage others well.

Whether for yourself or when hiring or promoting staff, you need to cultivate your ability to get work done through others. You have to be able to motivate, train, nurture, and discipline. Not everybody is comfortable doing these things.

Many people aren't good at making decisions, either. Some move too quickly, others too slowly. Many don't consider the repercussions of a yes-or-no decision.

Decision-making is an art as well as a science. Watch people who get things done. Critique yourself. And remember, non-decisions are decisions, too.

YOU PROTEST TOO MUCH

Often, those who say how much they hate a specific behavior are the ones who engage in that very same behavior.

When they state over and over that they are transparent, it often means they are not.

When someone claims they're not a micro-manager, they probably are.

Shakespeare's famous line, "the lady doth protest too much, methinks," has come to mean that when someone insists something too strongly, then the opposite of what they're saying must be true.

To build trust, don't give off mixed signals. From your management style to interpersonal communications, from accountability to resourcing, you must learn, grow, and evolve your personal brand with consistency.

The leadership lesson is simple:

Be consistent in what you say and what you do.

INFLUENCING OTHERS

Today's marketplace often manifests itself via non-traditional power structures. In a recent monograph, Jim Collins, author of *Good to Great*, makes a point of distinguishing between executive and legislative leaders. Executive leaders have the hierarchal power to make important decisions, while legislative leaders must rely on persuasion, trust equity, and shared interest to enable decision making.

Shorthand: *even if you are the boss, people may not listen to you.* You need to be able to persuade people.

There has been enough business dialogue on the distinction between managing and leading, so let's skip that. Anyone with good ideas and the ability to influence others can display leadership, regardless of their position in a hierarchy.

Obviously, persuasive skills are not limited to the CEO. Operational responsibilities generally fall on the shoulders of senior and middle managers. The collective leadership of these managers keeps their companies on course. Their style of execution is important, but so is their ability to communicate with, motivate, and manage their teams.

Our culture overemphasizes charismatic leaders—it puts too much weight on verbal skills and not enough on thinking and knowledge. If you are one of the quiet ones, you have to be able to convey your point of view.

Develop an arena of expression that works for you. A good idea that isn't shared is useless.

KNOW YOUR STRENGTHS

Size is frequently the measure of success in our society, yet a huge number of successful leaders work outside of large organizations or function below the top echelons. Success is just as relevant to them as it is to the CEO.

To me, success is accomplishment—but a broader term, and one that is currently popular, is the word *purpose*. Economic considerations aside, we all have intrinsic needs and values that have to be addressed, and being part of a group and doing work that excites and challenges us on a regular basis contributes to our personal success.

Recognizing your own value and demonstrating it convincingly to others is the real measure of success.

Organizational leadership requires a blend of individual and team strengths. So, what are the strengths required for success? Are they learned or inherent? Are they habits, skills, values, characteristics, behaviors? Their exact category or definition is unimportant, but you must display a set of team-building strengths in your professional life.

Professional success is also tied to fit. Not every place will be a match for your skills and talents.

If you're not being utilized, then look for something else. Life is too short for you to be miserable.

HOW SELF-CONFIDENT ARE YOU?

You need self-confidence to succeed.

You need to know your strengths and how to articulate your accomplishments. You have to look out for yourself. You can't expect others to do that for you.

Many managers, especially women, believe that if they work hard, others will recognize their accomplishments, and they'll be rewarded. This is a big mistake.

Focus on your achievements rather than your failures. Don't dwell on the negative, but every time you make a mistake, review it to see what you did right and what you would do differently next time. Learning from failure turns a negative to a positive.

Ask for help. Invite feedback. Say focused. Be positive. Set realistic goals. Take action. Do all of these things, and you can actively feed your sense of self.

IT'S IMPOSSIBLE TO PLEASE ALL THE PEOPLE ALL THE TIME—AND YOU SHOULDN'T WANT TO

You need to be likable to get ahead. People prefer to work with people they like.

But there is a dark side: being *too* likable. If you find yourself trying too hard to gain approval, to be accepted, or you act out of fear of letting someone down or being rejected, then you may be a people pleaser.

People pleasers want everyone to like them. There's nothing wrong with trying to make a good impression, but trying to get everyone to like you is impossible. No matter what you do, some people will like you and some won't.

Frankly, trying to make everyone happy means you may come across as disingenuous and manipulative. *The real you is the best you.*

People pleasers will do just about anything within their power to avoid displeasing other people, especially their bosses. They often feel like they have to say yes when someone asks for their help. If you are a people pleaser, then you may end up doing more than your share of the work, even when you are already drowning. It means that people may take advantage of you. Learn when to say no.

Being nice also becomes a problem when you fail to deal with a situation because you are avoiding confrontation. Interpersonal conflict is something we all prefer to avoid, because it makes us uncomfortable, but problems often get worse instead of better when left alone. Do not shy away from having a difficult conversation, just be careful about the time, place, and desired outcome.

There are many times when I have had to change the way I communicate with key colleagues, even if it means extra work for me—for example: talking and texting instead of just emailing, sending recap notes and extra reminders to keep projects and relationships on track, allowing for three follow-ups, not one. I have apologized when maybe I didn't have to. I have given credit when maybe I didn't have to.

Develop constructive habits for managing processes and initiating difficult conversations.

SOMETIMES YOU HAVE TO
STATE THE OBVIOUS

"The elephant in the room" refers to a situation when something major is going on, something on everyone's mind and impossible to ignore, but nobody talks about the "elephant," because nobody knows what to do about it.

It often takes courage to talk about an "elephant" problem. It also takes skill to address the elephant as well as to speak truth to power. You're on the other side of that coin when you are the one in power; be open to both inviting and listening to truth.

Another skill to cultivate—one that makes you even more valuable to have around—involves determining the not-so-obvious: a shift in direction, a mistake, changing alliances, emerging trends, unrecognized talent, etc.

To truly own this skill you need to listen, observe, learn, network, and reflect. Contrary to popular belief, your ability to be discerning isn't spontaneous; it's based on deliberate behavior—behavior that you can develop.

Invest time in growing your ability to see and understand events and behaviors.

COPING

My sister says I have good coping skills. Some days, I'm not so sure.

At what point does being supportive risk becoming an enabler? Does "biting your tongue" represent being tactful or being a doormat? Does offering another point of view mean that you're judgmental? Does working hard mean not working smart?

As always, it is a matter of balance, and balance is affected by environment and context.

Ask yourself some basic questions. *Is this a job I want to keep? Do I fit in? Do I need the promotion, or can I go elsewhere? Is there a pattern to my behavior? Do I need to change something about myself? Am I suffering from burnout?* (Hint: two signs of burnout are feeling cynical or ineffective.)

Basically, you can do one of two things: you can change the situation, or you can change your reaction to the situation.

You have to figure out what's important to the people around you, and then you need to decide what is important to you.

The everyday reality is that difficult people are all around you, and most people don't realize how problematic they are. To deal with them, you need to focus on things that you can influence and avoid expending a lot of energy or time worrying about people you cannot change.

Of course, coping isn't just about challenging people. It's also about coping with change. Change is a normal, natural part of our lives. What people do not like is someone else's idea being foisted on them, and what we tend to *really* not like are surprises.

You can make a situation worse by railing against it, or you can learn to accept it. It's up to you.

WHO EXACTLY ARE YOU?

Everyone develops a personal brand that distinguishes them from other employees

What is yours? Are you the nice guy? The prodigy? The pain-in-the-ass guy? The fella with good ideas? Are you the late-to-every-meeting gal? Or the on-time-but-say-nothing person? The smart aleck or the smart one? A good motivator of people or the micro-manager? The know-it-all? The contrarian? The quiet one? The best one for the job?

Your behavior determines your brand. Generally, the cumulative effect of your day-to-day behavior creates the impression of your style and substance to your subordinates, peers, supervisors, clients, and vendors. *So, be careful.*

Another thing to consider, as you look around at those who are achieving managerial success, is that many of them are strong personalities.

If you determine that you want the top-dog position, then you may have to ratchet up your personal style. Personally, I don't suggest becoming a S.O.B., but it's your decision to make.

Jim Collins' description of a level-five leader in *Good to Great* sounds wonderful, but I have to say that I have encountered far more senior executives who come with a large dose of arrogance, even obnoxiousness, rather than the humility Collins highlights.

I would like to acknowledge that not all top dogs are bad. Not all are oblivious or insensitive, insufferable, or egoistical.

Unfortunately, many leaders get lost along the way. The same strengths that propelled them forward can lead to negative behaviors. Be mindful as you move forward that this doesn't happen to you.

HANG ON TO YOUR SOUL

My favorite graduate class was a course on ethics. What was interesting to see was that the students with work experience were more engaged in the precepts and conversations than the straight-out-of-college students. I think it was because many of us had seen examples of questionable behavior in our day-to-day work lives—not outright fraud or gross immoral behavior, but misrepresentations and mistruths.

Presentations of performance successes (think curriculum vitae or resume) and investment and sales pitches often include elements of embellishment, which is generally considered good salesmanship. Critiquing competitors and internal teams to determine business advantages and gaps are commonplace activities, unless they are used to start rumors or sabotage a rival. Sales incentives and ranked performance reviews are standard business tools, *even when these practices can easily lead to misrepresentation.*

Misconduct often starts with small indiscretions. You take the day off and don't log the hours. You take returned merchandise home. A vendor invites you to vacation at his beach condo because, after all, you are friends. You ask a junior teammate to run errands for you. You justify the behavior to yourself. *You work harder than most others, you deserve it.*

You blame a colleague for a mistake you made. You make derogatory comments about a competitor to your client. You take credit for someone else's idea. *Others do it.*

Your boss harasses an employee and asks you to vouch for him or her. You see someone using undue influence, but they aren't really doing anything wrong, or are they? *You feel uncomfortable speaking the truth.*

The reality is that minor misdeeds can turn into larger ones—that is the slippery slope. Instead of passively looking the other way, you become an active participant in untruthful behavior.

Competitive workplaces are stressful, and sometimes shortcuts seem attractive. Guard against get-along or self-promoting behaviors that could erode your morals.

Part of your move-ahead strategies should include a focus on maintaining honesty, integrity, and respect for others.

WHAT'S YOUR ACHILLES' HEEL?

Everyone has one—a weakness despite one's overall strength.

The best workers, managers and executive leaders are not invulnerable—even the people you think are awesome. The specific flaw may vary, or its consequences might be amplified because of a particular situation or the people in the room.

Your Achilles' heel may not be immediately obvious, but that doesn't mean you don't have one. Sit back and analyze what you think it may be.

There are obvious traits like temper, recklessness, or hesitancy. What are some others? There's one that I've seen several times throughout my career: *loyalty.*

Loyalty to others—coworkers, subordinates, vendors—is an admirable strength, especially in today's disposable economy. But as with any strength, it can also be a weakness. Your trust in someone based on your experience of five years ago may not be warranted today.

The greatest strength/weakness that I encounter over and over again in smart people is that *they are smart.* They end up believing they are *the* smartest ones—and they often aren't—and then they become very poor listeners.

This blind spot, this inability to see or confront the skills that no longer work for you (or in the people you surround yourself with) will inhibit the trust that others have in you. It could also rob you of achievement and competitive advantages.

28

How to counteract this weakness? *Always try to include a few people in your orbit who will tell you the truth.*

Also necessary is a willingness to acknowledge the issue and then the desire to confront or adjust your situation.

Turn to your harshest critic to identify and evaluate what issues you may need to address.

TRANSFORM YOURSELF

It's never too late to be who you might have been.
—George Eliot

This familiar quote is both simple and true.

It's never too late for justice. It's never too late for thank-you notes. It's never too late to try something new. And it's never too late to change something about *yourself.*

At any time, you can take positive action that will add more meaning and value to your work or personal life, but you must want it badly enough that you will actually modify your behavior.

People often have trouble believing that they need to change something. *Are you negative at work? Do you instill fear? Do you procrastinate? Are you a tactless communicator?* It can be difficult to admit that perhaps there is a better way to do something that you *think* you have been doing well all along. Remember, your greatest strengths are also your greatest weaknesses.

Another adage: *the skills that got you where you are may not be the ones that will keep you there.* As your responsibilities change, make sure you take the time to evaluate your behavior. The classic example is that of a shoot-from-the-hip entrepreneur who started the ball rolling but is not suited for the next stage in the business cycle.

As your responsibilities change, check to make sure you are also evolving.

CULTURE CLUB

One of the biggest determinants of success is not skill set, but culture.

Culture covers a range of tangible and intangible behaviors. It can overpower new leaders, new processes, and new equipment. Have you heard the expression, "culture eats strategy for breakfast"?

Don't underestimate organizational culture, and don't overestimate your ability to change existing patterns.

You may need to adapt your behavior to fit in. That includes work hours, communication style, meeting cadence, transparency, risk tolerance, and more personal things such as attire and social engagement.

It is up to you to determine how much of an organization's "cultural Kool-Aid" you will drink.

SMILE

Be civil to all; sociable to many; familiar with few; friend to one; enemy to none.
—Benjamin Franklin

The idea of being nice is pretty simple.

Negative comments cause animosity and frustration with whomever you speak. Why create issues just because of your delivery?

It isn't always possible to follow the old saying "if you have nothing nice to say, then say nothing at all," because you often need to respond to situations with alternative points of view. But you can be constructive, educational, and respectful.

Will you have a bad day and say something you shouldn't? Of course, we are human, after all (just remember to apologize).

Serious, conscientious, hard-working employees are a treasure, but they aren't always fun. They may even be uncomfortable to be around if they don't laugh or smile very often.

Have you ever worked with someone who knew how to use self-deprecating humor effectively? Someone who liked to laugh and always had a smile? Someone who could walk into a room and release tension with a joke or funny comment?

Try to look for the funny side of things when your work isn't going as planned. Laughter helps build camaraderie among colleagues when the chips are down.

Laughter and happiness really are contagious, so if you're laughing, other people may join and make your workplace seem a lot happier.

I am not suggesting that you become a social butterfly if that's not who you really are. Let's just say, simply, that a smile is something nice to see, and it doesn't cost you a cent.

Projecting positivity will get you further than being viewed as a negative force.

YOUR PS AND QS

You must equip yourself to succeed.

Today's workplace involves collaborative, team-oriented tasks. You have to make individual and team performance meaningful and productive. You need to know when to give people space, when to work face-to-face, and when to share ideas electronically. Your challenge is to maximize everyone's contributions and minimize the potential for frustrating, inefficient group dynamics.

The colloquial expression, "minding your Ps and Qs," is used to encourage someone to pay attention to the details of what they are doing. It probably derived from the printing industry as a suggestion to be careful, especially when handling the lowercase *p* and *q*, since typesetters viewed text backwards when they set type.

I want you to use "minding your Ps and Qs" as a mnemonic aid for leadership smarts, as a shorthand for success strategies, because so many of the qualities that characterize a great manager are strengths that start with the letters *P* and *Q*.

The following *GET NOTICED* essays highlight these strengths.

Mastering these strengths will make you visible—in a good way.

EARNING MONEY IS NOT YOUR REAL PURPOSE

To have *purpose* means to be part of something larger than yourself—to help solve a problem, to lead a team, to deliver a service. It is to know that you make a difference to colleagues, to customers, and to the organization you serve.

Having purpose is a strong intrinsic motivator for many people. Charles Garfield wrote *Peak Performers* in 1986, a book that profiled top achievers from all walks of life. He identified a sense of personal mission as a primary component of their success.

Having purpose can include being productive, creating something, completing assignments, and supporting others.

I know the president of a family-owned business who orchestrated the buyout of another company that was ten times the size of the original. This David-and-Goliath leader (boy with slingshot beats giant) exemplifies a small force overcoming a larger one. I think his purposeful cycle of achievement is one reason he is so successful. He sets, at a minimum, one goal to be accomplished every day. Objectives range from large to small, but his key point is the establishment of an ongoing habit of identifying an objective and then achieving it. (If you adopt this practice, you will be able to acknowledge fulfillment at the end of the day instead of feeling oftentimes that your time and energy were wasted.)

All leaders have purpose. Their personal paths and styles vary, but they all have self-defined standards to meet, whether for their life's work or just for a particular time and place. Can you articulate yours?

PROTECT YOUR TEAM
AND YOUR BOSS

Look to the best interests of your team and your organization. Let them know that you will stand up for them. Shield them, not blindly but with open eyes.

Ensure that the people you represent know you have their interests at heart. However, have the courage to take corrective action when necessary. Your staff needs to know that you hold them accountable for their performance.

You can't expect people to believe you care unless you show that you do.

Realize that you need to demonstrate consistency. Nothing is more demoralizing than when your team sees inequity in disciplinary actions or promotional opportunities. Nowhere is the phrase, "perception is reality," more relevant. Be mindful that conclusions are often based on feelings, not on factual evidence.

When dealing with a problem, it's easy to make the mistake of appearing unsupportive of your subordinates. Preventing this impression can be difficult, because at the outset you don't always have all the facts. You can't appear defensive to either party, but if your staff experiences you as not there for them, you risk losing their trust.

This brings to mind a practice both simple and well-documented: *reprimand in private.*

Public censure causes, at best, individual embarrassment, but, at its worst, the demoralization of the entire group. You can easily damage a person's self-esteem and confidence when taking corrective action, so be careful.

Protect your supervisor as well as your subordinates. Is this sometimes difficult? You bet—but you need to demonstrate loyalty.

If you have a major disagreement, make sure you make the other party aware of it as soon as possible—but again, do so in private. I will say this more than once: it's okay to disagree, but you need to demonstrate that you are part of the team, and that includes working with your boss.

My father used to tell us that it was all right to squabble, but to keep it in the family, and this is also true in management. *Outwardly, always present a united front.*

If you can't support your company, your boss, or your team, then rethink your position.

Sometimes, due to workplace pressures, people feel that ethical principles are relative, open to interpretation, or subject to a philosophy that says look out for number one.

Don't fall into the trap of telling your boss what you think he or she wants to hear; build a trusted counselor position by objectively telling them what they need to hear.

Showing integrity in the workplace demonstrates soundness in your character. Don't do anything you think is wrong.

PASSION IS CARING ABOUT WHAT YOU DO

By *passion*, I mean zeal—zeal for outstanding performance and zeal for the work itself.

Passion is not merely a "soft" attribute. Have a strategy to build or maintain it within your organization or department, because passion will bolster motivation, encourage teamwork, and provide a foundation from which to strive for excellence.

Entrepreneurs apply their passion to their vision for their businesses and reap the rewards. Nonprofit organizations depend on passion. Employees and volunteers work for these organizations because they believe in the cause. However, this passion must be nurtured, even in places that allow you to match your heart to your skill, because the work can range from being overwhelming to downright tedious.

I know an extremely talented and caring woman who managed the HIV/AIDS work for an international charity. A key focus of her work was caring for those living with AIDS. Caregivers who do this work witness so much death. Without their passion and faith in the mission, they would not be able to function, because the pain would be intolerable.

You need to make sure that passion is a key operating strategy, and you must keep that passion alive both in yourself and others.

ALWAYS HAVE A PLAN B

Being *proactive* means thinking ahead.

Some environments are naturally chaotic. That doesn't mean you have to be completely reactive in these situations. The expression, "controlled chaos," can be used to describe police stations, newsrooms, construction sites, and even restaurants. These are places where external variables and erratic schedules are ever-present.

You can be proactive even in frenzied environments. Plan ahead, empower others, and use a little common sense.

However, if your position or your personal style has resulted in you being rushed more often than not, realize that you can break the habit of being reactive.

The more senior your position, the more often you are thrust into a reactive mode. This is especially true if you have created a culture where you have delegated decision making to lower management levels, because it means the issues you are engaged in tend not to have been resolved at lower levels.

Create an activist atmosphere with the objective of trying to stay ahead of problems by anticipating them. What if something works too well, or if it doesn't work at all? Are you prepared? Have you constructed realistic schedules, set contingency plans, built operating margins, and invested in crisis management, employee training, and succession planning?

Are you creating a work culture that enables employees to do their best and learn from their mistakes? Or do you play the blame game? Forensic reviews are great, because they help you say, "That happened last time, and now this is what we are doing differently." Just be sure to focus on the solution, not the fault.

Many people disparage themselves when they say, "I covered my butt," and then go on to explain how they documented something or created an extra copy *just in case*. I consider this to be proactive behavior and encourage staff to think about what may go wrong and then find ways to recover from a particular situation.

Now, this strength of anticipating different outcomes can be carried to an extreme and become a weakness, especially if it turns into "I told you so" instead of "this is how we can fix it."

When it comes to communicating bad news, being proactive is the best strategy. *Defense is the best offense* doesn't apply only to sports.

Telling someone bad news before they find out from others or before they ask about it is an excellent way to build trust. It also helps you control the conversation. So many people postpone or procrastinate when it comes to conducting difficult conversations, and that can make the problem worse.

You should be the one to inform your supervisor about a mistake or a problem. Don't bury it or have a subordinate deliver bad news.

It's natural to dislike controversy, but avoiding controversy can become a significant weakness. Problems rarely solve themselves. Avoidance normally leads to larger problems, and it can actually cost you the respect of the person(s) involved.

Preparing for future possible problems is just plain smart.

STRENGTH IN NUMBERS

I always work on creating and empowering strong teams. Building *esprit de corps* really is the best response to change, stress, and tedium. It is another proactive strategy.

Invest time in developing trust and respect. Allow your team to understand one another's strengths and differences. Let them have fun as they learn to work together. They will respond by helping each other.

If you have interpersonal conflicts within your team that you haven't been able to resolve, consider using a mediator to help you and those involved understand and modify each other's behavior. *It's okay to ask for help.*

Two ways to develop strong teams are:

Delegate decision making whenever possible; this encourages the quick resolution of problems. Delegate as much decision making as possible, but build in simple reporting mechanisms so you are apprised of problem issues. I once worked for someone whose mantra was, "I don't like surprises." She was right.

Don't fall prey to "big company disease" with its endless meetings and unnecessary management practices and policies. (Big company disease manifests itself by frustrated talent who leave and start small companies that are then bought by big companies, the same big companies that originally stifled their innovation.) Nothing stifles teamwork like bureaucracy.

You are ultimately judged on the strength of your team. Be sure you make it as strong as possible.

INVEST IN PEOPLE

How many times have you heard someone say, "People are our greatest asset?"

Many companies talk about the importance of human capital, but I have seen very few actually act in a way that supports that statement.

Today's reality is that materials and even technology are cheap and easily acquired, which means sustained competitive advantage is most likely to come from the ingenuity and motivation of a company's employees. There should be investment in recompense, training, and educational support for *all* employees, not just executives.

Being concerned about *people* should also include fostering an environment that balances professional and personal time and actually encourages time off. Burned-out employees have limited long-term value, and the employees most likely to develop burnout tend to be your best employees. They usually put more of themselves into their jobs, spend more time at work, and take their work seriously and personally.

Make sure you are not trying to do too much with too little. It is all right to ask your employees to give 110 percent, but not every day. We all try to maximize limited resources, but make sure that your organization or operating unit is staffed appropriately.

Study the cost of turnover and dissatisfaction. This could change your mindset the next time you establish salary grades or make benefit and manpower decisions.

Set a goal of improving the performance of all those engaged in making or selling your products and services, especially the frontline representatives of your organization.

Employee development is a critical building block to organizational success, and it represents a proactive culture. Make investments in growing knowledge—for everyone, not just a few selected superstars.

Don't take a hands-off approach to understanding your team's dynamics. Human beings are messy, and you can't depend on rules and procedures to manage and motivate them. A team is truly only as good as the people it keeps.

THE BEST OFFENSE IS
A GOOD DEFENSE

Risk taking, for me, is a critical element of being *preemptive*. Taking risks is also intertwined with innovation.

Look at Intel's publicly communicated values for risk taking—they are the keys to product innovation and market success:

- Foster innovation and creative thinking
- Embrace change, and challenge the status quo
- Listen to all ideas and viewpoints
- Learn from our successes and mistakes
- Encourage and reward informed risk-taking.

These are great corporate values. They can also apply to you as an individual.

Developing a reputation of looking ahead, of being curious and willing to try new things, puts you in the *she can see the forest for the trees* camp—meaning people will recognize that you can see the big picture.

Make it easy for voices to be heard in your group. Be flexible. Adopt an "innovation by accident" attitude. What does that mean? When a mistake is made or a customer asks for a custom application, don't mire the issue in bureaucracy. *Evaluate the process and the desired outcome.* You may end up with a new product or be on the way to streamlining a process.

Change can signal success. Or, perhaps it is better to say that change provides *opportunities* for success.

Being preemptive also means helping your boss. *Consider the key priorities your supervisor needs to accomplish.* Take the time to anticipate his or her pressures. Would accomplishing your goals advance your boss's priorities or inadvertently conflict with another team that reports to him? *Tie your work to the larger goals of the division.*

The higher you go, the more time and effort you need to expend in understanding and helping your supervisor. *Remember, no one is a mind reader.* You need dialogue, even if you have to initiate it.

If you have a bad boss, you need to come to terms with that relationship. Criticizing him or her either publicly or privately will not help you. Either deal with it or move on.

Make proactive, informed decisions, balancing both risk and reward.

ALWAYS LOOK FOR TALENT

One of the hallmarks of a leader is the ability to recognize and nurture talent.

I like to be around people who are smarter than me—it keeps me on my toes. That includes people who report to me.

Your staff is the greatest reflection of your abilities. If they are strong, you are strong. Look for people with *potential*, look for people who can do your job. Why be passed over for a new opportunity because no one else can assume your current duties? You have to prepare someone to take your position.

Take risks with subordinates. Let them stretch. Assign them special projects. Give them access to other managers and departments. Give them access to your boss. Hand over additional responsibility. Allow them to fail. However, be advised that *stretch* doesn't mean abandoning them without support. The old-school attitude of, "I've paid my dues, now it's their turn," really doesn't work.

When recruiting, enlist peers who have built strong teams, and use them in your interview process. Some people have a natural talent for interviewing, so tap into that ability.

Listen to your inner voice. There are plenty of fish in the sea, so don't rush your decision. The next candidate may be the best one.

Today's emerging values center on life-work balance and personal engagement with work. *Construct opportunities for employees to play significant roles.* This will appeal to people who want to be involved and who seek meaningful work.

Lead by example. Your employees should always know that you wouldn't ask them to do anything that you wouldn't do yourself, but that doesn't mean you have to do what they do. You will have greater impact—and get more done—if you teach and mentor them.

Hiring someone smart doesn't mean going after over-qualified people for positions with limited growth potential. They will become bored and dissatisfied. That dissatisfaction will spread because negativity breeds negativity—exponentially, in fact.

Always be on the lookout for talent. This doesn't mean poach people from other organizations or departments, but let people know that you're interested if they ever want to make a change.

Don't hide the talent on your team. Encourage you team members to apply for opportunities throughout the organization. Become known as a grower of talent.

An effective workforce is a key competitive differentiator. Help attract, nurture, and retain talented people. Doing so is one of the best ways to stand out.

ACKNOWLEDGE THE EFFORTS OF OTHERS

This is so simple, but we always seem to forget it. *Praise* people. *Say thank you.* Tell employees, whether they are on your team or not, that they are doing great. Do it publicly and privately, and always with sincerity. A few sincere words of praise are invaluable. And don't forget to praise your boss.

The other part of praise has to do with matching employees to opportunities that will let them be their most successful. Read *Now, Discover Your Strengths*, by Marcus Buckingham and Donald Clifton. Instead of focusing on weaknesses and allowing strengths to lie dormant, they suggest identifying and building on strengths to achieve success.

This doesn't mean you should ignore weaknesses, but stay aware of where you will reap rewards. *Find situations that fit your capabilities.* If you are precise and thorough, consider being in a place or position that allows you to concentrate on details. If you thrive on challenges, be in a place where you can handle difficult assignments. If you are a good listener, build on your ability to nurture relationships. If you cannot stand the boredom of routine, find a position with variety.

Do the same for your staff. I really don't remember when the light bulb turned on for me to focus on strengths instead of primarily addressing weaknesses (dressed up as coaching), but it made all the difference. It became easier to identify work opportunities and to promote and develop people when we focused on their strengths.

People are at their best when focused on work that is important to them. Help people identify opportunities that fit their skills and motivations.

KNOW WHAT IS POSSIBLE

Possibility should be grounded in reality therefore *practical* is one of the most important *P* words. To me being practical means exhibiting a combination of strategic and executional skills. If you can't "land the plane," then all the great ideas in the world aren't worth the paper they were sketched on.

I am continually surprised at the emphasis we place on strategy and the lack of emphasis on execution. Occasionally, one sees good execution of a bad idea, but sadly, the norm is poor execution of a good idea.

The real measure of success has always been about deliverability. That's not an original thought, but you must marry strategy with tactics and then be able to move from the theoretical into reality. Action theorists believe that execution is an essential part of the creative process. That's been my real-life experience as well.

Good practitioners are able to figure out what's needed to accomplish a goal—including human capital, technology, and time, as well as evaluating risks and identifying obstacles.

It means being optimistic, but you must guard against being overly optimistic. That can be hard, since it's the positive projections that get the proposal approved.

Many plans are built mainly on internal variables, but *you have to pay attention to external variables*. Articulating the "threat" section in a SWOT (strengths, weaknesses, opportunities, threats) analysis too often becomes an academic exercise. Congratulations if are someone who adjusts your plans when variables change.

Being realistic means being grounded. Can you recruit qualified people in the next two months to start a new project, if your track record is really six months? Can you really close new sales next quarter when the standard development cycle is twelve months? What happens when fuel costs dramatically increase, or a competitor changes their pricing?

Successful leaders can translate idealized concepts into present realities. They know how to overcome obstacles, to plan ahead, and to empower staff.

Good managers have mastered the art of decision making, knowing when to move quickly—or conversely, when to slow things down—when to confer with colleagues, and how to learn from mistakes.

Are you familiar with Edward de Bono and his six hats? De Bono has identified six thinking strategies and uses colored hats to describe each unique viewpoint. He encourages the deliberate use of all of them instead of the two or three that an individual or team might naturally drift towards when making decisions.

The de Bono hats include:

> *The White Hat focuses on the facts. Looks at trends. Looks for information gaps.*
>
> *The Red Hat looks intuitively and emotionally at the issue and considers how people will react.*
>
> *The Black Hat looks critically at the issue and evaluates why things might not work.*

The Yellow Hat takes the optimist's view and allows one to see the benefits of moving forward.

The Green Hat manifests the creative perspective. Brainstorming and freeform thinking goes on here.

The Blue Hat represents process, and the wearer of this hat makes sure all the thinking hats are employed.

This technique is fantastic, and it provides a framework for a well-rounded development and review process. It encourages emotion and skepticism, and it allows for contingency planning and creative leaps. It also sets the stage for collaboration and helps slow the process down—enough, at least, to think through all the issues.

De Bono's hats also help guard you from being too optimistic, a common pitfall when promoting a new idea that leads to unrealistic expectations being set. There's nothing worse than being known as the guy with the unrealistic ideas or the projections that never translate into reality.

My advice is to not oversell the results, while avoiding underrepresenting the risks.

Build trust by sharing the range of possibilities.

DON'T BE NEGATIVE

People react to your moods, so watch what you say and do. If you are negative and grumpy, they will be, too. You set the tone, and that tone almost always becomes apparent. Be *positive* (without being a Pollyanna).

This applies to outlook, not just style. People respond to optimism.

It pertains to self-talk as well. That's the constant stream of chatter that goes on in your head. Through this internal dialogue, you make decisions, set goals, feel happy or sad, hopeful or lost. Do you constantly criticize yourself inside your head? Do you constantly criticize others?

Self-talk conversations can be about failing. Athletes are particularly vulnerable to this. They all have slumps—times when the harder they try, the worse it gets.

Setbacks happen. Mistakes occur. Evaluate what took place, and then make peace with the situation. Don't dwell on it. Mike Ditka, former professional football coach, has said, "Success isn't permanent, and failure isn't fatal." And while that isn't quite true, because many professionals actually do risk injury and death, winners understand that you will lose your edge every once in a while. But how you react and adjust to a mistake or a decline in performance can keep you from a full-fledged slump.

Stephen Covey talks about positive energy enlarging circles of influence in *The Seven Habits of Highly Effective People: Restoring the Character Ethic.* He advises people to work on things they *can* do something about, instead of focusing on weaknesses and circumstances they have no control over. Negative focus results in reactive language, blaming, and feelings of victimization and negative energy all which cause circles of influence to shrink.

You can never be successful if you believe that you are a victim, and it is almost impossible to seek opportunities when you are defining yourself as part of the problem.

Recently I heard someone utter the phrase, "It's not my problem," and I listened to her tone. Instead of thinking "lazy," "irresponsible," or "uncooperative," I realized this was one of the healthiest expressions one could ever hear.

A balanced, proactive response to a problem involves first evaluating whether the issue or difficulty you have observed or learned about is inside or outside your sphere of influence.

If you see a problem in your workplace, with a volunteer activity, or even in your family life—and it is not within your purview—then I urge you to leave it alone. This doesn't mean turn a blind eye; but to be successful in your work life, you have to decide how to best use your time, energy, and talents.

People frequently worry about problems they cannot possibly impact. Additionally, they complain about the issue to others and, by doing so, unintentionally become part of the problem. Sometimes the worst offenders are an employer's hardest-working employees and volunteers. Conscientious workers take their work seriously and personally. They fret about problems—all the problems—and they start to resent those who don't share the same level of concern.

It's easy for competent people to get involved in problem solving. It takes self-knowledge and some discipline, but you must learn to say, "It's not my problem," with confidence and know in your mind and heart that saying so is proactive and positive behavior.

I was offered some advice mid-career that has helped me when I thought I was stuck: *Compare yourself to yourself, and see how far you have come.* My other go-to is: *Listen to your gut.*

Your intuition is often right. Don't let too much doubt or enthusiasm get in its way.

LOOK OUT FOR YOURSELF

For some this is easy, for others it is more difficult. You have to *promote* yourself. That means you need to toot your horn when you have been successful. It's human nature to notice weakness, but don't expect others to notice success. Peers and supervisors are busy, and even your immediate boss doesn't notice your everyday successes.

This practice may be the single most important factor for not becoming invisible.

Competent and accomplished workers and managers make difficult jobs seem easy, so let colleagues know when a challenge has been met. Make sure you communicate about completed assignments; just be sure you're not arrogant.

Don't wait for others to notice you and your work. Share your good news.

Apply for selected promotions, and voice your interest in new opportunities. For self-effacing people, this can be difficult.

Get involved in trade associations and other in-house projects. Your supervisors and colleagues may believe you practice your craft well, but that belief can be strengthened when they hear endorsements from those outside the organization or not involved in day-to-day operations.

Networking is important, and you should do it every day. Think of it as good "career hygiene." You have to intentionally invest time in networking. It doesn't really take a lot; the key is regularity, like flossing after meals. Stay in touch with former employees, bosses, and vendors. After reading articles that you like, send a note to the author. Call friendly competitors and ask for advice.

Build a personal network that can help you with future endeavors. This network can be an important community for right now and can help you feel connected, provide feedback, and gain knowledge, all of which will increase your current value.

BECOME A GOOD PUBLIC SPEAKER

If you're not a natural speaker—and many of us aren't—then you have to *practice*. Practice out loud. Practice in front of a mirror. Practice in front of your team. Soon, you will get to a place where you won't have to practice any more.

I once had a boss who told me that he never made a bad career decision. What an optimist! (I learned that what he really meant was he took advantage of every situation, whether or not it seemed to be the right move, by developing new relationships or learning new skills.)

At one time I worked for an advertising agency that was not a good match for me, but I benefited from its belief in the power of effective presentations and its willingness to develop those skills among its employees. "What's Your Point," by Bob Boylan was one of the best courses I took. I hated that job, but I've been grateful every day since for the formal training I received.

If your firm won't spring for a public speaking or media training class, consider doing it yourself. I can testify that it will be one of the best investments you will ever make.

ALWAYS LOOK FOR SOLUTIONS

Leaders are often the chief *problem solvers* in their area because of their technical knowledge, interpersonal skills, the depth of their professional networks, or their positions of authority.

One mark of a leader is that he or she will make decisions, often with limited information, and accept the consequences.

Some managers are intuitive, others analytical. A great differentiator is the ability to commit. Don't be so afraid to make a wrong decision that a decision is never made. You will never hit a home run if you don't step up to the plate.

Simplicity is an essential goal. Work toward simplifying your organization's structure, measurement systems, and rules for decision making. Reduce distractions and focus on a handful of principles and practices that can make critical differences in performance.

When dealing with a problem, a tendency toward complication can sometimes lead to solutions that are more burdensome than the original problem. Focus on identifying and streamlining the issue. Try to break it down to a few essential truths.

Don't be afraid of making rapid choices. Malcolm Gladwell in *Blink* discusses first impressions, prejudices, conscious and unconscious attitudes. Good decision-makers learn to be wary of historical associations and stereotypes—for example, that attractive people are trusted more—and they control their first impressions in order to make quick decisions.

Don't be afraid to acknowledge when a mistake has been made.

The ability to commit does not mean you must decide in a vacuum or make a series of unilateral decisions. An artful combination of fortitude and skilled consensus-building is what's most often called for. That doesn't mean managing by consensus, but actively working on *building* consensus.

Become proficient in conducting collaborative conversations. This doesn't mean asking for input and then completely ignoring it. You don't have to take the advice you get, but close the loop by explaining your thinking and interpretation.

Identifying an issue before it becomes a huge problem is another important aspect of problem-solving. Be cognizant of small things that may be symptoms of something larger. Don't sweat all the small stuff, but look for patterns or other systemic problems.

And be sure to keep your perspective: do not let problem-solving become your focus. Problems never, ever close sales, develop new products, or create cool marketing insights. Even if you are proficient at resolving issues, you won't get a seat at the table unless you can tie that talent to growing the business.

Remember, offering solutions is always more successful than offering criticism.

DON'T GIVE UP

Perseverance means not stopping the first time you hit a roadblock. It doesn't mean becoming inflexible or refusing to see the unavoidable, but it does involve recognizing that change takes time and effort. New ideas need fine-tuning. New teams need time to acclimate.

Ever heard of Robert the Bruce? (Think *Braveheart*.) After being beaten by the English in battle six times, Robert, King of Scotland, was a fugitive. According to Bernard Burton's poem *Bruce and the Spider,* one night he watched a spider as it repeatedly tried to spin a web:

> *The patient insect, six times foiled,*
> *And yet unconquered still;*
> *And soon the Bruce, with eager eye,*
> *Saw him prepare once more to try*
> *His courage, strength and skill.*

Bruce took courage from the spider's perseverance and tried again a seventh time. This time, he finally succeeded in defeating the English.

Another quote, one by Mary Anne Radmacher, recently caught my eye; it speaks of resilience and hardiness (an old-fashioned term, to be sure). It speaks of spirit:

> *Courage doesn't always roar. Sometimes courage*
> *is the quiet voice at the end of the day saying, 'I will*
> *try again tomorrow.'*

MANAGE YOUR TIME WELL

There is *never* enough time. You have to *prioritize*.

Effective managers figure out how to triage, how to keep small things from turning into large problems, and how to keep big projects moving. They know all tasks are not equal. They know they can't read every memo, make every hiring decision, meet every customer, or solve every dispute.

When you lack the ability to focus your time, you don't just burden yourself; you also disenable your staff. So, it's better for everyone if you delegate.

To impose order onto chaos, we often revert to tasks we know we can control. I know a manager in an organization facing severe financial challenges. He is an engineer by trade, and if the water cooler or air conditioning breaks, you would find him in the thick of it. He enjoys the hands-on problem solving and probably needs the distraction. For a couple minutes of therapy, this is okay, but make sure you limit activities of this kind.

Always gauge your use of time by asking: *Am I the only one capable of performing this task?* There are relationships and decisions that only *you* have the responsibility to handle. So, most of the time, do what only you can do, and let others do their jobs.

If you are blessed with a great memory, congratulations. Otherwise, keep lists, use software, or hire an assistant or manager to keep things on track. It's all about being organized (and that doesn't mean being neat). It's about managing the hundreds of micro-decisions that we have to make each day. The keys to success lie in your ability to juggle, delegate, and follow through.

Another part of prioritizing is actually beginning. As Mark Twain put it:

> The secret of getting ahead is getting started. The secret of getting started is breaking your complex overwhelming tasks into small manageable tasks, and then starting on the first one.

People procrastinate. They research. They talk. They just don't always start.

I advocate using the bottom-up approach—I've used it over and over again—when trying to clean up a piece of business, absorbing new work, or getting a new team organized.

It means starting with day-to-day activities and commitments. While many advocate a "work from the top down" approach, the fact is that if you can't get the day-to-day under control, you will never have time to focus on larger issues. And it's the larger issues that matter more in the pursuit of real change and ultimate success.

So why not start there? Again, it is an issue of effectiveness. If you can't get the daily obligations under control, you will never get to the larger issues. You'll stop and start too frequently as you get pulled back into dealing with daily issues, and you'll be forced into a reactive mode. Then, for the big things, you will be forced into rushing them.

I'm not saying don't think about big things. Just master a couple of things at a time, starting with the everyday, and then you can plan when to tackle the large issues that have likely staring us in the face for a while. Frankly, most of what we do is not rocket science, but what we do does require thoughtfulness and follow-through.

Once you get the day-to-day things under control, the stress relief alone will give you a sense of freedom that will inspire you as you tackle big issues and take on new projects. Just don't stay in the world of small problems.

STOP AND THINK

Because we are so busy, it is easy to always *do.*

But you need to *pause,* to deliberately set time aside to think. It will increase your creativity, improve your listening skills, and help you be less reactive.

This need for time applies not only to you, but to your staff as well. We all need downtime. This time could be at the office or outside it, in formal or informal settings. It might be individual time or group time, like no-meeting Fridays.

Thinking needs to be part of your ongoing work culture. You need time to be creative, to look ahead, and to foster innovation. To help keep things fresh, I recommend Robert Sutton's book, *Weird Ideas That Work.* (My favorite section advises, "reward success and failure, punish inaction").

Creativity takes hard work. Try R. Keith Sawyer's book, *Explaining Creativity: The Science of Human Interaction.* His hypothesis is that people who are thought of as creative work hard at it. Creativity has to be nurtured. Innovative and creative thinkers spend a lot of time generating ideas, thinking about problems, and coming up with potential solutions. They also get involved with other creative, like-minded people, learning and sharing together.

I absolutely agree. Creativity isn't spontaneous.

The best way to have a good idea is to generate a lot of ideas, so make time to think.

STOP AND LISTEN

You can't manage well unless you understand your employees' motivations, and you can't *really* gain consensus unless you understand their feelings. Since we're not omniscient beings, we learn by listening and observation.

Good communicators know the importance of listening. Do you listen carefully, quietly, and effectively? In our eagerness to communicate our own thoughts, we often forget to listen.

Show genuine interest in what others are saying, but don't be a passive listener. Ask questions and seek clarification. Look for verbal clues. You can be a better listener when you *look* at the other person. Listen in a way that demonstrates understanding and respect. Ask questions, instead of giving your opinion. Try to understand others' points of view. Focus on the conversation, and don't get diverted by other tasks (like talking and texting at the same time). Put down your phone and be present.

Part of the foundation of influencing others is the ability to establish rapport and common ground. *Listen as much as possible.*

A good listener will fight distractions and poor communication habits and figure out how to concentrate, while a poor listener will just tune a speaker out.

Don't forget to pause for a reply. One of my most annoying habits is that of interrupting people as they speak. It's rude, and it's especially unfortunate because it belies the fact that I actually do listen.

Another key pause moment is when faced with a disciplinary action or decision that will affect a person's livelihood. I'm a pretty quick decision maker, but I do maintain the discipline of waiting a minimum of twenty-four hours before making a final decision about an employee. You need time to gather the facts and consider the implications. Listen to both sides.

Don't rush to judgment.

DON'T ACCEPT THE STATUS QUO

A prudent question is one-half of wisdom.
—Francis Bacon

It is good to *question.* It encourages discussion and debate. Probing questions help people flesh out ideas and issues.

My advice to you: Ask questions throughout your professional career, but remember how important it is to ask the right ones.

Be sensitive in choosing when and where you ask your question. You are likely to be ignored or dismissed if you ask your question in a forum where it's off-topic; or if you pose a very elementary question when advanced questions are expected, or vice-versa.

Don't ask a question if the sole intent is to make someone look bad.

You need to encourage people to express their opinions and ensure that all parties involved are heard. In groups, sometimes only a few people participate in discussions. It's important to help those who may not feel comfortable to speak up. You need to make sure that a variety of perspectives are explored. Inviting alternative ideas helps get more people into the conversation.

Do you remember how hard it was to ask your first supervisor a question? Remember to make it easy for your staff to approach you.

If you were boss for a day, what would you do? Ask this question of your peers and subordinates. It will be a goldmine of useful information. Yes, you may get some off-strategy ideas with the "boss for the day" exercise, things that have been considered and discarded for a variety of reasons, but what a simple way to get the pulse of your team, to obtain new ideas, and to get support for changes in direction.

One of the most significant things that happens to leaders is that they get insulated. Do you remember the fable *The Emperor's New Clothes?* Just because your boss (or your boss's boss) believes something is true doesn't mean it is.

Develop techniques for soliciting feedback. Don't fear or resent comments. Instead, actively cultivate getting input. It will make you better at what you do.

No one is right all the time. If you are in a position of authority, many people will not be comfortable challenging you. If you're an expert or have loads of experience under your belt, people tend to automatically believe that you're right.

Of course, the most important thing to guard against is *you* actually believing that you're always right. The step past *being* right is being convinced that *you are* right. It is hard to know when one has become self-righteous, when one has moved past the point of learning.

Work to create a culture where everything is open to question. I suggest that you regularly say, "I'm not always right," and "What do you think?" This behavior leads to faster problem solving and increased creativity and productivity. *Try it.*

The best way to prevent errors is to have multiple people looking at something from different points of view. I try to involve people with various levels of experience and different specialties as a way to encourage innovation as well.

If you have a forceful personality, it may put people off. Teach yourself to be more restrained and not to criticize, but to help guide arguments. Doing so will help win people over to your ideas.

Remember that it's okay to disagree; the key is to do so agreeably. Is that difficult when you're passionate about something? Absolutely, so watch your tone and body language. Never make the issue personal.

Be careful not to become the only questioner. If your work culture doesn't support this level of engagement, then do not become the bad cop unless your boss specifically asks you to assume that role—or else you will have become visible for the wrong reason.

My advice to anyone in a position of authority: stay grounded. Don't become the naked emperor. That is a kind of visibility, or invisibility, you want to avoid.

READ BETWEEN THE LINES

You can observe a lot just by watching.

—Yogi Berra

Some of the best bosses are able to hear what is not explicitly stated, to ask the question behind the question, and to see both side of an issue. This *perceptive* ability can transcend experience and often requires more than good analytics; it requires understanding for the other person or position.

Listen for what is *not* being said.

Be cognizant of the fact that others may interpret what you say and do in a way that is different from what you intended. It is human to see what we want to see and to believe what we want to believe.

An axiom to keep in mind: *Before you judge a man, walk a mile in his shoes.* This old adage is a call to be less judgmental, to foster understanding, and to encourage empathy.

Pay attention to words, tone of voice, gestures, and facial expressions.

Keep an open mind and look beneath the surface.

DON'T PLAY FAVORITES

An awful lot of personnel disputes arise out of perceived favoritism or inconsistent applications of workloads and benefits. *Parity* can be hard to achieve, because our world is rarely black and white but is instead made up of infinite shades of gray.

From the *Principles of Marine Corps Leadership* comes a great definition for *justice*: "Justice is the giving of reward and punishment according to the merits of the case in question; the ability to administer a system of rewards and punishments impartially and consistently."

Does this mean you should not make exceptions? *Of course not.* Does parity conflict with the idea of motivating and responding to staff members on an individual basis and tailoring your approach to their personal strengths and weaknesses? *No.* The principle is one of equality and fairness, not an imperative to make carbon copies. Personalities, situations, and requirements vary greatly. The same solution will not apply to every situation.

How do you know if you are achieving parity? *Solicit feedback from staff. Pay attention to exit interviews. Ask peers for their observations. Ask your supervisor for input.*

This is an arena in which it is easy to think you are being fair, but it may not appear that way to others. Not everyone can know all the facts, and many situations involve confidential information.

Your employees have to believe that you're being straight with them. Be as transparent as possible without breaking confidences. Those who believe you aren't fair could become your biggest detractors.

PARTNER

Is this a win-win, win-lose, or lose-lose scenario?

A genie offers a farmer one wish, but whatever he chooses, his neighbor will get double. The man sits and thinks about it for a while, facing the dilemma that anything that benefits him will make his neighbor twice as fortunate. One hundred camels for him means 200 camels for his neighbor.

"Poke out one of my eyes," the man responds.

It's an obvious *lose-lose*. This genie joke addresses a rather negative view of mankind: even if the situation benefits us as well, we don't want to give anyone an advantage.

In sports, one side wins, and the other side loses. I hate the fact that a team has to lose (ask my family, I always root for the underdog). Yet watching a team actually work with each other, whether it's little league or the major leagues, is a joy. When players work together, teamwork demonstrates that the whole is more than the sum of the parts.

I believe in win-win scenarios. Creating them is often easier said than done, because the principals often look to maximize their own advantage.

I know an extremely capable woman who has been professionally rewarded at every level. However, she approaches every encounter as an adversarial relationship. She often creates short-term gains, but others frequently have to counteract the long-term impact of her win-lose outcomes.

The concept of *partnering* helps lead us to create win-win or positive-sum outcomes.

Partnering means working together—*reciprocity.* It means sharing knowledge and responsibility. It results in advances in problem solving, creativity, innovation, and speed.

Partnership is not without challenges. It requires a willingness to give up some control, and it also means you have to rely heavily on effective communication and defined roles and responsibilities. It requires trust.

Collaborative habits are learned. Start by delegating decision making whenever possible. This practice encourages the quick resolution of problems by the people most directly involved. Process and procedures shouldn't be intentionally ignored, but you must realize that too many rules and regulations can stifle an organization. A good leader knows when to make an exception.

One of the worst things you can do to an employee—any employee—is to micromanage them. It took me years to learn to restrain my controlling tendencies and not inflict them on my staff. I hate being micromanaged, so how can I expose others to that?

The higher you rise in an organization, the less effective you will be if you hold onto negative control habits. Micromanaging signals distrust and a lack of respect. How can you build a strong team if your behavior belittles your group's contributions?

A healthy collaborative relationship with vendors means that they will succeed when you succeed. Help them be successful. Don't be miserly with information. Not all vendors are partners, however; some are simply suppliers. There's no need to call a relationship a partnership when it isn't.

You will be occasionally disappointed with partners because something will go wrong—but give them a second chance. Walk away if the mistakes continue. There are plenty of potential partners to take their place.

If you pay someone for a "thinking" work product, then don't constantly second-guess or ignore them. I will never understand why a client will pay an advertising agency to develop an ad and then change the font, the colors, the pictures, and rewrite all the copy. Either rely on their expertise or do it yourself.

> *"If you have an apple and I have an apple and we exchange these apples, then you and I will still each have one apple. But if you have an idea and I have an idea and we exchange these ideas, then each of us will have two ideas."*
> —George Bernard Shaw

Joining with other like-minded or complementary organizations in order to reach a goal is a great way to maximize resources and minimize risk. It may mean that you need to give up some control, but you may reach a goal faster, reduce overhead, or limit redundancy.

Recognize that by working with others, you may be able to accomplish more. That will make you more valuable.

FULFILL YOUR OBLIGATIONS

Have you watched the 2000 movie *Pay It Forward?* It is a story about an 11-year-old boy who starts a project of practicing kindness and compassion, and it contains an empowering message of possibility, of change.

What does this have to with business? How do you apply the idea of *paying it forward* in a professional context? To my mind, it represents the need to develop trust and the importance of building community.

Community provides a sense of belonging to a group with shared values that can provide reinsurance; better still, that community can yield advocates for you.

Your staff, your peer group, your customers, your vendors, even your competitors are all part of your community.

You must actively work on building trust equity. It will help you when something goes wrong, or if there is a misunderstanding, which there inevitably will be. I don't mean that everything has to be a *quid pro quo*, but proactively looking to help others will pay off well in the future.

Another way to explain community comes from *A Year in Provence,* a made-for-TV version of the book by Peter Mayle, based on his real-life experience when he and his wife left their jobs in England and acquired a farmhouse in Provence.

Peter develops an obsession for boules and resolves to beat the local champion. He builds a court, he practices, and he takes lessons. He is determined to beat this guy. Another ex-pat finally says to him, "I can help you win."

And Peter did win—by losing. The question posed was, "What do you want to win?" For Peter, it was to be accepted by the villagers, to not feel like a foreigner. By losing to the champion, he became part of the community, and thereby he won.

This charming lesson illustrates that building community will be key for your success.

You don't have to win every encounter. Be thoughtful of the possible outcome before you take a hard stance.

CONTROL HOW YOU
HANDLE STRESS

Poise under pressure is a good way to get noticed, whether in reference to crisis control, an ongoing stressful situation, or some form of management conflict.

Sometimes a public crisis can propel someone into the spotlight, but we will all operate at one time or another in a taxing situation. That situation could be an event or a cumulative set of experiences or a pervasively negative workplace culture.

What do you do when stressed? Yell? Forget to say thank you? Skip steps, skip meetings, miss deadlines, make mistakes, miss meals? Just one of the above? All of the above? Do you become nasty and put on a few pounds from too much junk food?

The key is to assess how you react to stress. Do you attack, or do you withdraw? Do you actively try to minimize that tendency when you're tired or upset?

Try to stay calm. Invite input while you evaluate. You can show emotion, but you need to project confidence. Stay focused on your strengths.

Projecting a combative stance is a problem. Don't let the first question be, "Whose fault is this?" Instead, focus on fixing the problem. Debriefs can happen later.

In his autobiography, Ben Franklin talks about how "disputing, contradicting and confuting people are generally unfortunate in their affairs. They get victory sometimes, but they never get goodwill, which would be of more use to them."

Sometimes you will lose control of your temper. It is inevitable. If you do lash out, acknowledge your lapse in behavior and apologize.

Treating others with respect and dignity may be at odds with the reality of your corporate culture. High-sounding mission statements don't always translate to corporate actuality.

The mark of a real leader includes treating *all* people with respect, deference, and politeness. Unfortunately, there are many who reserve that treatment to those with lofty job titles and treat those without them with disrespect. That reflects rather poor character, don't you agree? Consider how obvious that behavior is.

Remember: "What goes around, comes around."

PAIR UP

A "hit pair" in the moviemaking business is a pair of lead actors or performers who appear together in several different endeavors. Abbott and Costello may be the most famous of them all—the devious straight man and the dimwitted laugh-getter, the ultimate yin and yang.

Co-leaders are an interesting phenomenon. They are more of an exception than the norm in today's business environment, although they are not a modern-day invention. You can find them in ancient Rome, when Caesar and Pompey ruled as co-counsels. However, since they were bitter rivals, they don't quite represent the co-leadership model.

One form of co-leadership is a forced pairing. A board can't make a decision, and so they split responsibilities between two people: not always a recipe for success.

More interesting and successful, however, is when two people actually complement each other and their outcome is more than the sum of the two individuals taken on their own. Often, they themselves initiate the pairing because they know that they need each other to be successful. It requires both a strong sense of self and a measure of humbleness to acknowledge that perhaps you are not the best at everything on your own.

I have had the opportunity to see several of these types of peer business partnerships work, and I am fascinated by them. They work because the principals trust each other.

Most frequently, this kind of pairing takes the form of a leader supported by his or her number two. We witness arrangements like this in action when we see an introvert work with an extravert to provide a balance of temperament, or when an analytical guy matches up with a creative guy, or when one plays the role of internal cheerleader while the other becomes the outside salesperson.

Can you find someone with whom you can partner in a way that the two of you can propel each other further together rather than apart?

BUILD SPHERES OF INFLUENCE

"Absolute power corrupts absolutely."

Although this phrase is often attributed to Machiavelli, it was actually coined by Lord Acton, a British statesman. We reflect on it whenever we hear about someone who has fallen after they reach the ultimate pinnacle of success.

Losing your moral compass is significant, but this axiom applies to everyday behavior as well. Misuse of *power* doesn't apply just to corrupt or callous leaders; it also applies to insular leaders.

Many people in positions of authority become shielded and lose their ability to see what's important. Don't believe your own rhetoric or surround yourself only with people who tell you what you want to hear. Be careful that exception-making behavior that your position permits doesn't become your norm.

You may think you have the pulse of the people, but your leadership responsibilities set you apart. You may have to remind yourself that you are not "one of the guys." You need to figure out how to stay in touch with employees, because they can help you remain grounded.

When you have a leader with clout and influence, you can observe another dimension of power. Clout is positive for a team. A team needs someone who is an advocate, who can effect change, and who can garner needed resources.

I worked for a wonderful boss once. He was smart, he set high performance standards, yet he was reasonable in his demands. However, he had no standing with his boss, and as a result we were always under-resourced. We were the low team on the totem pole, and that made it impossible to sustain any level of success. In that scenario a boss with influence even if he or she had some leadership deficits might have been the ticket to our group's success.

Effective leaders are able to provide their employees with the authority, knowledge, and skills to complete their mission. I remember sitting in on a sales pitch one time, and the president of the company said, "It is my job to give the team the tools they need and then to get out of the way." It was the smartest thing I ever heard him say.

Sometimes using power well means simply being a buffer. Buffering means looking out for the best interests of your team and your organization as well as absorbing criticism and distractions.

Many of us have a negative reaction to the word *political*. We think of manipulation, insincerity, or exploitation. Yet leaders need to be effective at influencing others—the positive sense of the word is "sphere of influence." *You need to build this at every level.*

Keeping lines of communication open requires work on your part. You need to foster an environment in which people can constructively challenge each other. Forget the employee suggestion box. Instead, stop and talk to people one-on-one. I also suggest you mentor several younger people. Among other things, they will give you the skinny.

I'm a great proponent of informal communication. I hate perfunctory staff meetings. Still, group meetings can be useful forums for sharing information. If you have the courage, an open meeting is a way to invite dialogue. Your job is to keep the discussion on point and productive.

Getting issues out in the open is the fastest way to stop the "gossip grapevine." However, creating a place where employees feel safe can be difficult. You may want to start with small groups. Success will come slowly. You have to build trust.

The size and speed of the gossip grapevine indicates the degree to which your official communications are poorly organized. *Remember, you can positively impact communication in your areas even if the rest of the organization is dysfunctional.*

I believe people want straight talk all the time, especially employees.

Poor communication is a systemic problem in most companies, big and small, old and new. Generally, the problem consists of a lack of information and lack of trust. Employees are not dummies—honest dialogue and approachability mean a lot. Don't put off talking about bad news. Don't sugarcoat it.

I know that trying to get a message across to every employee in an organization is a lot like herding cats: some will listen, some will hear but misunderstand, and some will ignore the message altogether and later say, "Nobody told me."

Despite the pitfalls, work to build transparency by being as open as possible.

Finally, don't forget that another form of power can be expressed as simply empowerment. If employees have the ability to take on more responsibility and authority than has been given to them traditionally, then give them more power. Operational leadership, to succeed, must ensure that employees understand what to do and that they are provided with the authority, knowledge, and skills to do it.

Evaluate who has power and influence in your circle. Work to build your own assets of positive power built on trust and reliability.

YOU NEED LOTS OF IT

"Patience is the companion of wisdom."
—Saint Augustine

Patience comes up frequently for many people when they are asked to identify an area in which they would like to see personal improvement.

I think we all want to get projects completed quickly. The trick may be in knowing when to appreciate the process and not shortchange the schedule or steps needed for a positive outcome—to *not* show irritation when something is moving slower than we want it to, or if someone makes a mistake. Patience takes practice.

Improving one's patience may be one of the most difficult aspects of business self-improvement to achieve.

SYNTHESIZE

People have short attention spans. We are conditioned to the sixty-second sound bite and the ubiquitous PowerPoint presentation.

Long presentations and meetings are almost always boring and rarely conducive to learning. It turns out that many, many speakers are actually poor communicators.

Learn how to paraphrase. *Work on making your messages brief. Simplify the issues and the solutions, and be sure and make the information relevant.* Franklin D. Roosevelt once told his son, "Be sincere, be brief, and be seated."

Tailor your delivery to your audience. You should have a core message, but what you say to customers will have different points of support than those you would invoke when talking to with employees, investors, or other constituents.

You always have to answer the unspoken question your audience is unlikely to vocalize: *How does this affect me?*

Get your answer down to just one reason—the reason why they should listen to you or do business with you.

MEASURE WHAT YOU DO

Many people distrust numbers. They don't understand them or suspect that the numbers given to them have been manipulated. But it's hard to make good choices when you have no *quantitative* information.

Numbers help you navigate biases and opinions. Numbers have helped Mark Penn, pollster and author of *Microtrends*, develop and defend winning counterintuitive strategies for politicians and business leaders.

Don't become simply a data collector. You need to understand the intelligence your data represents. Count both quantitative and qualitative things. In the service world, I like client satisfaction scorecards. Clients answer a range of soft questions over a host of topics like service orientation, responsiveness, business documentation, resources, quality, strategic vision, and value proposition. The exercise is useful for the client, because it gets them to actively review and articulate how they actually feel about the service or product. And it's helpful in matching our perception of our service to theirs.

Don't fall victim to analysis paralysis, either, calling for more data and failing to make decisions.

Successful managers are not afraid of performance accountability.

DON'T BURN YOURSELF OUT

I am a great believer in momentum and moving quickly. Ennui is the enemy. Besides, energy is fun.

I have seen projects sizzle with energy. Approaching deadlines can sometimes ignite creativity. Conversely, deadlines can extinguish creativity if managed badly or if rush projects become the normal work mode. *Pace* yourself and your team.

I have seen ideas turn flat or fizzle because people get tired of them. One thing that can happen when you have too much time is fiddling—getting input from so many people that you lose the idea's original force.

Once again, balance is the key. Ideas are strengthened by others; they can also be diluted by others. It has been said that the key to failure is trying to please everyone. You may be familiar with the saying, "A camel is a horse designed by committee."

Speed is part of our lives. Technology and globalization are making the world go even faster. If you don't plan to arrive at your destination quickly, others will get there sooner.

There are many different places to inhabit in the marketplace, and following the market leader might be an acceptable strategy for many industries and products. But make doing so an intentional strategy and not just a knee-jerk reaction to getting there late.

Maintaining a worthwhile pace also means taking care of yourself. Take breaks, and don't overwork yourself to the point that you become ineffective because you are tired. Evaluate your schedule and your overall time management.

Remember, don't just work hard, work smart. You have to guard against burnout. Conscientious people need to be especially careful. It's easy to volunteer for projects, and that can lead to taking on more than you should.

My first significant career lesson was learning when to say no. I was working for a data management company, and we were converting our largest client's multi-million-record database to new software while simultaneously managing a very heavy schedule of catalog mailings. My customer service team absorbed the added efforts of learning the new data structure and conducting system testing, all while carrying the existing workload. That was our corporate culture.

One piece of programming code out of thousands of lines was flip-flopped, and the value it represented affected the information needed by the post office to deliver the mail. Millions of catalogs were rendered undeliverable.

After the fact, it was so easy to see that additional staff was needed. Just one person dedicated to quality control would have made the difference.

Learn when to say no.

Why do you keep saying yes? Are you looking for affirmation? Are you not comfortable or secure enough to say no?

Have you stopped to consider the cost of the work that you just absorbed? These costs include loss of personal time, increased possibility of mistakes, the chance of getting overwhelmed, and missed opportunities.

You should always work to maximize the time you have, because time is your scarcest resource. It's easy to get distracted from your core responsibilities or your career plan. Taking on one too many new "opportunities" is a way to lose focus and not advance.

Let me emphasize that it takes skill and courage to know when to agree to accept additional responsibility and when not to. To be frank, pissing off your boss may not give you the kind of visibility that you are looking for.

BE YOURSELF

People follow people.

Loyalty is almost always directed towards people. Supervisory relationships are crucial in determining employee satisfaction levels.

You don't have to be the most popular, but people need to be able to connect with you. Coworkers and customers, especially in today's collaborative workplace, favor likable employees and supervisors.

Don't try to be someone you aren't, but do not let being "professional" rob you of your *personality*. Bob Dole, when he was running for President of the United States, came across as dull and stiff, and yet he was a genuinely funny man.

Let your personality shine through whether you are an introvert, extravert, or ambivert (a cross between the two). Play up some of the strengths of your natural personality, which could be your wit, good-ol' boy demeanor, maternal nature, creative spirit, or whatever else sets you apart.

Consistency is also important. Having a great boss one day and a not-so-great one the next day is awfully hard to deal with.

Be careful about your ability to be sociable with subordinates, because it can blur the lines of authority. Not many people can go clubbing one night and then conduct performance corrections the next day.

Don't become known as *just* the nice boss. The best bosses aren't the ones who let their employees leave early, chitchat with them about their family vacation, or look the other way when a small mistake is made (although you should do all these things occasionally). The best bosses are the ones who hold you accountable and help you grow professionally.

Don't become a tyrant. My best professional advice to one of my siblings was, "It's okay to be a hard ass, but not an asshole." Abusive behavior exacts a toll.

There has been a lot of talk recently about toxic leaders. They are awful, and you have to guard against becoming one of them.

I believe the most dangerous leaders are the ones who don't want to hear bad news, and you don't have to be toxic to fall into that category. The dysfunctional culture that results from telling the CEO only what he or she wants to hear can severely damage a company.

As you rise through the hierarchy, make sure you are approachable enough to hear what's going on.

CONVINCING OTHERS

You must be able be *persuasive* as you communicate your point of view. Almost every business dialogue is about attempting to effect a change of some sort, getting a customer to complete a purchase, coaching an employee, or presenting a new idea to your boss.

Beyond informing, you have to motivate. The most successful persuaders focus on making participants feel comfortable about making decisions and then helping them act on them.

Evaluate your own personal style. You may be analytical, or you may be more expressive. Then place your style in the context of your organization or compare it to the style of the person to whom you're trying to tell your story.

Ask a mentor to help you communicate more effectively, or ask a colleague to critique your participation in meetings.

Always remember to make any presentation a conversation. The objective is to engage the other side.

A simple question that may help you evaluate your communications skills: *Are you an interesting lunch companion?*

Conversation is one of the most habitual and ordinary things we do, but it's also one of the most creative things, because of the natural ebb and flow of the dialogue and its unexpected twists and turns. It can be a real learning experience.

Conversations are a great way to learn from others as well as share your own knowledge with them. Virtually every relationship we have partakes of conversation at its core.

With that in mind, *Can you put people at ease? Can you converse well about a range of topics? Conversely, have you ever had the experience of exchanging preliminary pleasantries with someone and then hardly saying another word?*

Some people are naturally sociable. Many others struggle because they just don't quite know what to say.

If you get seated at a table where you don't know anyone, introduce yourself to the person next to you. Ask questions, and get the other person talking. To be a good conversationalist, you must discuss topics that are of interest to the group, so keep up with trends and current events.

If you are an introvert, this might be hard, but it's a skill you should develop.

An effective conversationalist will spend most of his or her time listening. *Ask questions. Smile. Look at the other person. Don't worry if you have lulls in your conversation. Finally, be tactful.* We often hurt other people's feelings by not being sensitive to their circumstances.

The following email has been floating around for a while (this was before social media was the norm). You may have seen it before. I find it a captivating way to illustrate the power of language and remind us that the words we use shape perception.

> *One day, there was a blind man sitting on the steps of a building with a hat by his feet and a sign that read: "I am blind, please help."*

A publicist was walking by and stopped to observe. He saw that the blind man had only a few coins in his hat. He dropped in more coins and, without asking for permission, took the sign and rewrote it.

He returned the sign to the blind man and left. That afternoon the publicist returned to the blind man and noticed that his hat was full of bills and coins.

The blind man recognized his footsteps and asked if it was he who had rewritten his sign and wanted to know what he had written on it.

The publicist responded: "Nothing that was not true. I just wrote the message a little differently." He smiled and went on his way.

The new sign read: "Today is spring, and I cannot see it."

I sat through a meeting the other day and was once again struck by how lousy most organizational leaders are at tailoring their message to their audience.

Core messages and values should be the same across all constituents, but don't give an external message to an internal audience. It comes across as irrelevant, boring, condescending, or all three.

Effective managers are good communicators. They have figured out how to be persuasive.

Be authentic, be clear, and keep it short.

Be open to other points of view. It's okay to change your mind. Not being able to change it actually warns others that you're becoming too rigid.

Don't vacillate either. One manager I know is always influenced by the last person to talk to her, and that's a leadership problem. Those of us who work with her can't get a sense of her vision, since her path reflects so many different points of view. (The same was said of Czar Nicholas II, and remember what happened to him.)

Once a decision is made, even if it isn't one that you originally supported, keep your mouth shut. You should remain part of the team. Don't tell everyone you disagree, or that you would have done it differently.

This was my second significant career lesson: Pay attention to what your organization wants to hear. If they don't want to hear the truth, then don't drive yourself insane trying to tell them.

Words matter. In fact, they become representatives of you and your values.

INVEST IN PEOPLE

Quality usually denotes some degree of achievement and is usually contrasted with *quantity.*

Successful leaders invest in quality, especially in quality people. Both Jim Collins and Peter Drucker, the two undisputed management gurus of our generation, have written extensively on this subject.

The quality movement of the 1980s generated the term, "total quality management." TQM is usually a company-wide initiative that focuses on satisfying the needs of your customers by utilizing standards higher than those of most of your competitors.

One result of TQM is an emphasis on measurement. However, it isn't algorithms that create quality, but people—people who are empowered to solve customer problems or to stop the production line when they spot a problem. People who are encouraged to create new things and to take risks.

Organizations that receive quality acclaim have created cultures that support employee engagement and communication transparency.

Build healthy work cultures.

TRY NEW THINGS

Being the first to try new things is an excellent way to get noticed, and it's also an effective way to stimulate change and develop new ideas. A little variety and stepping outside your comfort zone can help you avoid stagnation in both thinking and performance— both for you personally and for your team. *Become known as a progressive thinker and implementer.*

Integrating new procedures, technologies, and overcoming resistance fundamentally involves a *people issue*. Most people are uncomfortable with change—at least at work. People don't mind change if it's perceived as effortless and good. We love new cars, TVs, clothes, furniture, etc., but in the workplace we don't like mistakes, doing things over again, and extra labor.

Know who you can call on your team or in your network to help execute change. Communication is critical. Implementation often falls short because people were not appropriately involved or informed. Communication is also linked to your workplace culture.

And culture almost always trumps strategy. It can often be hard to describe a company's culture, because it's intangible, and at times it's even ineffable. You can't see it, but you can *always* feel it.

Some workplaces are welcoming. Some are obstructionist. Others are smart, inventive, or social. Some are bureaucratic. Some are serious, and some are chock-full of energy.

Over a decade ago, "culture" was cited as the reason—or excuse—for Penn State's response to its headline-grabbing sex abuse scandal. It's clear that, sometimes to a horrifying extent, culture can blind us to what is front of us. It can generate selective perception all too easily, and so information gets ignored if it conflicts with the company view or management's fear.

I know a firm where the senior executives were so hell-bent on impressing the CEO that no one managed down—all they did was manage up. It was a sure recipe for finger-pointing and front-line employee burnout, and in the end the real losers were the clients, because the work was sloppy. Not a surprise, because the firm's energy was not focused there.

A company's tone can be set by the top dog or by the next level down. It can be set by tradition or held captive by legacy practices and relationships. It can also be maintained by inertia.

Changing a culture is difficult but necessary when a company's tone and mood affect its ability to do business well.

Often, those who dictate changes in the form of new policies or new organizational directions do not attend to people's predictable reactions with regards to disruption: apprehension and fear of the unknown. I suggest you try to truly understand your organization's culture, assess how employees might react to change, and then craft a program to provide support for everyone as you navigate the process.

If you want to become an effective leader, then take risks and accept responsibility for your actions and those of your team. Doing so sends a loud message to others about your capabilities, your integrity, and your strength.

In the Parable of the Talents from the *New Testament*, the master gave one servant five talents, the second servant two talents, and the third servant just one. The master then left the household, but he returned after a season to see what they had done. The servant who had been given five talents turned them into ten, doubling their value. The second servant turned his two talents into four. The third servant, however, buried his talent in order to save it.

Those who had increased their holdings were rewarded with more, but the master took the money away from the servant who had operated out of fear and done nothing.

I was introduced to the idea of a fourth servant in Michael Curtis Ford's work of historical fiction, *The Fall of Rome*. How would a fourth servant have been received, one who had been given several talents but lost them as a result of trying something new or taking a risk? One can speculate that he would have been praised and given another chance to learn from his mistakes. This take on the parable reinforces its idea that *failure is about not trying.*

Are you fearless? I'm not. I am self-reliant, sometimes bossy, analytical, and not afraid of change. I'm not afraid to fail, because in order to succeed you have to try things, and to try things, you have to sometimes fail. But I am not naturally fearless.

Some people are genuinely unafraid to pick up the phone and make a cold call, travel to a new city, or jump right into a new activity without a moment's hesitation. I envy those people.

Many people are uncomfortable with new people or new places or new things. They're scared of being rejected or of looking stupid in front of teammates. Well, so am I. But I force myself to do things I don't always want to do. It makes them easier to do the second time, and then the third time.

The point here is that at work, you need to figure out your risk tolerance and work to manage that—either rein it in or push it out. I often describe myself as a cautious risk-taker. I don't go simply with my intuition; I look for insights to support the pending decision.

My self-help advice is to put yourself out there the next time you feel uncomfortable. You may surprise yourself.

SHARE KNOWLEDGE

Good leaders share. It's an essential component of who they are. They don't subscribe to the old-school idea of hoarding information, instead they *part* with knowledge and share their time. They build trust, nurture talent, and encourage innovation.

Hoarding can be either a conscious or unconscious act of holding back—and not just information; this observation works for people, too. Encouraging people who have often been overlooked and excluded and providing them with incentives is an excellent way to grow organizational strength.

As organizations grow in size, geographical scope, and complexity, the need for shared knowledge and collaboration incubated though more formal structures grows. Be part of building knowledge networks to improve organizational performance by helping communities collect information and connect those with knowledge to those who need it.

Make it a point to be involved with helping members share and learn, both formally and informally.

You can help build bridges for people of color by recruiting, training, mentoring, and coaching, by providing access and opportunity, and by engaging communities through products, services, advocacy, and volunteerism.

It's smart to be indispensable. Hard workers are valued by their co-workers and their bosses. They show initiative and are reliable and knowledgeable. But is being indispensable the best way to succeed? One of the most serious dangers of this mindset is *thinking* that you're indispensable. That can lead you toward extremely hands-on behavior that communicates that you feel you must be involved with every decision.

Your ultimate success stems from your ability to influence your team's ability to accomplish the mission or tasks assigned to them. Your inability to delegate or let go of information actually disenables your staff.

You will have greater impact, get more done, and get noticed more often if you teach and mentor rather than relentlessly do it yourself.

BE READY

Napoleon Bonaparte's military success (well, up until his Russian winter campaign) was always marked by logistical *preparation*.

Peak performance is almost always linked to preparation, and this link is especially obvious in collegiate and professional sports. Coaches and athletes spend endless hours preparing for games— as do military units, medical professionals, and emergency service groups for their respective arenas of engagement.

So why do we wing it so often in the civilian world? We routinely employ junior staff in positions that they are not equipped to handle and justify it as on-the-job training. This bad habit is as prevalent in Fortune 500 organizations as it is in small businesses.

Managers around the world spend hours and hours writing policies and procedures, believing that doing so fulfills educational mandates. I'm sorry to have to say it, but posting documents to an intranet site is inadequate in terms of actual education, as is transmitting information orally to a passively listening audience.

We need to adopt some of the best teaching practices used in schools today, adopting approaches like:

Storytelling: Stories and metaphors make things easier to remember.

Assigned Tasks: Participants complete a task and compare results with colleagues.

Case Studies: Real-life examples are a memorable way to make studied topics more relevant.

Role Play and Simulations: Participants explore problems by enacting them and then discussing the enactments.

Understanding that people learn differently is fundamental to teaching. Some can absorb new information by listening, some by reading, and some by doing.

Policies and procedures are no substitute for active learning, and learning must be integrated into everyday practices and made accessible to the learning styles of your individual team members.

Preparation includes tools, not just training. Why hire someone to do a task and then hamper them with faulty equipment? I believe in operating "lean and mean" as a matter of principle, whether as a steward of donors' resources or stockholders' earnings, but I also believe in equipping staff with the basic resources to do their jobs with a minimum of hassle. Employees understand saving money, but they tend to get frustrated when computers, copiers, and heating and cooling systems do not work.

Filling positions with junior staff is an acceptable strategy if you have adequate training and consistent supervision. If you can't provide that, then change your strategy and hire more experienced people who don't require a high level of supervision. It's a pretty simple business model decision. The alternative is unsupervised junior staff, which is a recipe for failure.

Preparation includes personal learning. You should always be gaining new information and mastering new skills. Many people enjoy the process of learning. Others invest in academic or professional credentialing as steppingstones to new opportunities. Whatever your motivation, set learning as a personal goal.

I don't ever want to be *that* person—the one who always says, "We tried that before. It won't work."

Life-long learning in the workplace is a necessity, and active educational preparation helps make you more valuable.

Don't be a dinosaur. Don't be overtaken by events. You should always be learning new skills, meeting new people, and trying new things.

BE ACCESSIBLE

I am using the word *present* in the sense of "being at hand." In a managerial context, it represents the need to be accessible. Keep in mind that presence, in this sense, becomes another one of those key practices that becomes harder to fulfill as you rise in an organizational hierarchy.

At whatever level, you need to be both approachable and available. Figure out how to carve out time to make sure you can do this without overloading or compromising yourself. It's a fundamentally vital and effective communication strategy.

You can't ignore co-workers' requests for help and then fuss at them later for moving forward without you. If this happens repeatedly, it's *your* problem. No one, especially you, should blame it on your co-workers or subordinates.

Some people are not good at raising the red flag. They think they can handle a certain situation, or they don't want to bother a busy person with yet another demand on their attention. But if you are asked for your input and you don't respond, then what happens next could be the equivalent of *caveat emptor*—"let the buyer beware."

Even if your team isn't asking you, you *still* carry the burden of responsibility, because you have to make sure your team understands the kinds of issues that have to involve you. You need to continually reinforce the message, *Although I am busy, I have time for you.*

Some managers use the old MBWA method ("management by walking around") which can be adapted for today's remote teams. Others have special email accounts, still others set aside certain hours or days for employees to set walk-in or Zoom appointments. Many managers invest in being reachable by initiating contact with as many people as possible through one-to-one touches to see how they are doing. They call or text to keep the conversation more comfortable and less official.

Some managers use a surrogate approach and receive information by talking regularly with a few key colleagues or subordinates, effectively letting them function as their eyes and ears. This option is especially helpful if you project a more distant persona; however, this can keep you isolated so be careful.

I know a manager who was really intense at work, but luckily he recognized that about himself and worked to make himself more approachable. His solution was humor—and not humor aimed at other people, but self-deprecating humor. He got people to laugh and open up. He was still driven, but softening his edge let him become much more human and approachable.

Figure out a way to be approachable that works for you.

CAREER PLAN

I think the saying, "Find a job you love, and you'll never work a day in your life," is terrible. Work is work, and not all work is lovable. That's why we look for intrinsic satisfaction in other life experiences, from volunteering to hobbies.

Even people who have turned a passion into a career need to spend time practicing and improving their craft and performing tasks that, though they might not enjoy them, are necessary for success. Time management and career decisions are just as vital for zookeepers, ballerinas, and baseball coaches as they are for accountants and human-resource professionals.

Many middle managers end up being good at their jobs, but they don't love what they do, or else they no longer get to do what inspires them. Think of the art director who manages a team but no longer creates anything herself, the executive chef who expedites rather than cooks, or the senior law partner who no longer litigates.

Many managers end up using their annual performance reviews accompanied by the ubiquitous career development conversation as roadmaps for their careers. Since performance goals are largely oriented toward the organization rather than the individual, I believe that using them in this way is a mistake.

So, what exactly is career planning? It isn't simply having an endgame objective, although that's part of it. Fundamentally, it must focus on developing skills and pursuing opportunities. Career planning means knowing your core competencies and what makes you unique. Much more than being in the right place at the right time, it depends on impressing others with your knowledge and capabilities.

In order to be deliberate about your career movement and not just roll with the tide, you need to formulate a game plan. It should address your aspirations as well as include a communication strategy of how to effectively network in your field and make yourself sought after as an expert in it.

Career planning requires you to stay continuously alert to opportunities. In fact, beyond that, you should help create them. To be competitive both today and tomorrow, you need to follow current trends while thinking about the future at the same time. An approach like this helps you achieve a more desirable result: instead of taking the first decent job available, you develop a strategy for finding the right job for both right now and the future.

We constantly hear about a growing number of adults who are making mid-career switches. Many people do this because they're simply not passionate about what they do eight hours a day, five days a week, fifty weeks a year. Now, people seem to be making a conscious effort to fill the gap between their reality and their dreams. They crave a more fulfilling and meaningful work life, and so the closet authors, farmers, entrepreneurs, and artists begin reaching towards new careers that match their energy and talents.

I suggest you start today by writing down several personal and business goals, and that you include a few that relate to expanding your circle of influence or simply trying something new. What do you have to lose?

Not everyone can start over, but you can focus on what you enjoy doing most at work.

PBALANCE (THE "P" IS SILENT)

You need to maintain an equilibrium between your work and home life. Family and personal time should always be a priority, and there are plenty of activities outside the workplace worth your time. In fact, outside interests will allow you to perform better at work.

Indulge yourself by reading a book, traveling, or exploring a new hobby. Volunteer, coach a team, mentor a child, or sing in the choir. Make time for exercise—it helps with self-esteem and provides a sense of accomplishment.

Other life experiences will help you generate new work-related ideas, and the mental and physical distance from work will refresh and strengthen you, especially if your work life is not engaging or is negative.

Let's face it: miserable jobs hurt. Jobs you dread kill enthusiasm and generate cynicism.

Don't stay at these jobs, unless you think you can learn something, and then make sure you put a time limit on how long you'll stay.

BE VISIBLE FOR THE RIGHT REASONS: AVOID THESE TRAITS

Perfectionism
You will fail.

Just because there's no such thing as perfection doesn't mean you can't be terrific at what you do, or that you shouldn't strive for excellence. However, setting goals to be perfect will always lead you to disappointment. Plans and projects always need adjustment, and people will never live up to your expectations.

Perfectionism is a self-imposed burden that you should not try to carry. It will make you painful to deal with or just flat-out crazy.

Passive-aggressive behavior
Don't say one thing and do another.

Learn how to manage conflict in a positive fashion. Repeat after me: *Just because I disagree with you doesn't mean I don't like or value you.*

It's amazing how many people cannot separate addressing behavior in the workplace with personal value judgments. What is the benefit in telling someone who is constantly late that they are irresponsible? Better to communicate to them how lateness is a problem because it affects others and is therefore a behavior that must be changed.

Many people shun confrontation and endure substandard performance or uncomfortable situations because they lack confidence about handling disagreement.

Learn to constructively offer different points of view. Sometimes what we might call passive-aggressive behavior can be an ordinary defense mechanism. With a super-difficult work relationship, vaguely agreeing on non-critical issues can be a necessary tactic that allows you to keep going.

A pattern of saying one thing and doing another, however, is a severe problem. Once you're tagged with it, the passive-aggressive label is hard to remove.

Quitting
Fulfill your obligations.

Don't abandon projects, people, or jobs. Finish what you start, and end it well.

Pettiness
Overlook small slights.

An old-fashioned word, slights, but still relevant. Even if they drive you crazy, you have to let some of the small things roll off your back.

You don't always have to have the last word. Insisting on it causes others to question your priorities as well as your ego. You absolutely do not have to prove that you're the smartest guy or gal in the room.

Procrastination
Don't put it off.

Many people struggle with procrastination due to a lack of time management skills, stress, or the feeling of being overwhelmed by their job responsibilities. If a lack of necessary knowledge keeps you from getting something done, ask for help.

The flip side of procrastination, however, can be a good thing when done smartly. A delayed start can provide some useful time to think and allow you to broaden the idea, even change the idea and help you simplify the process. Taking some time to approach a project might let you unearth things that never really needed doing, so you can scratch them off your list in advance. A slower start might help you find the right team members.

However, more severely: if you put off important tasks, you could be doing your career harm, especially if a delayed start results in poor execution.

Pretense
People will see through you.

Don't pretend to know more than you do or take credit for someone else's work. It will eventually catch up with you.

Pawn (or Passing the Buck)
Don't pass off problem employees

Don't pawn your problem children off on other managers.

Make a serious attempt to let employees know the issues that might be blocking their road to success.

Your own inability to deal with confrontation may hinder the employee from changing his or her behavior. It certainly doesn't help subsequent managers who will have to deal with the situation that you have passed on, and it could damage your reputation.

PARTING ADVICE: BAD GUYS

There is always a bad guy. Sometimes it's a person, an organizational structure, or an external event.

Many reflect classic conflicts: headquarters vs. the field office, manufacturing vs. sales, sales vs. marketing. Or it could be a nasty client, an incompetent vendor, or a wacky boss.

Be aware of the bad guys, and consider how to respond. Sometimes you can embrace the situation. Natural tension might actually result in developing better products and services. This wouldn't be my first choice, but I also don't believe in get-along behavior that compromises quality.

First, identify the bad guys because, undoubtedly, they exist. Then figure out how to ignore them, neutralize them, or attempt to influence them.

It is hard to be on the defensive all the time, and that often happens with the bad guys. They either openly criticize or use innuendo. If you invest time in finding common ground, they could become an ally.

Ultimately, *it's better to be inside the tent pissing out than outside the tent pissing in*. My hands-down favorite quote of all time, by Curt Littlecott, points out the importance of working to engage, involve, or contribute however you can—anything to avoid becoming a target for criticism or attack. It probably means swallowing your ego. Ask others to help you figure out how to overcome obstacles.

It's okay to start small—remember *circles of influence*. These circles expand, and if you can help others, they in turn may help you.

Sometimes you can coexist with the bad guys. In fact, a bad-guy boss can make you look good, although he or she may make you feel miserable. Some situations, however, are not fixable, and the best option can be to accept things as they are and bite your tongue or decide to look for another opportunity.

It's about *your* coping abilities, and only you can decide if you can handle a difficult situation. *Focus on things you can influence.*

But perhaps above all: don't become the bad guy. Be the good guy.

Trust yourself—your work ethic, your empathy, your integrity, your knowledge and your resiliency. You got this!

Printed in the United States
by Baker & Taylor Publisher Services